# Pitching

# A Casual Fan's Guide

by
**John Yates Britt**

**Pitching – A Casual Fan's Guide**

Published by:
CFG Enterprises, LLC
Post Office Box 8125
Calabasas, CA 91372

First Edition Published 2016.

ISBN 978-0-9887233-3-7

# Preface

My first book, *Baseball – A Casual Fan's Guide,* was published in March 2013. In it, I focused on presenting baseball in such a way that people who knew little or nothing about the game could easily learn it. To that end, I created an imaginary game between fictional teams, and I took the reader through the game, inning by inning, explaining what was happening out on the field. Because I wanted to keep the book's focus on the game, I mentioned only four Major League Baseball ("MLB") players by name. The then-Director of Research at the National Baseball Hall of Fame's Research Library in Cooperstown, New York, told me that he was not aware of any other book where the author had taken this approach to explaining baseball. Moreover, I wrote the book in a conversational style, hoping that a welcoming tone would encourage folks who knew little or nothing about baseball to understand and appreciate the game that I love.

My approach was well received. A top-150 product reviewer for Amazon wrote, "I've flipped through the pages of more encyclopedic references explaining the game before, struggled with my gag reflex, and then put them back on the bookstore shelf. This Guide doesn't challenge my gag reflex and doesn't put me to sleep. It's well written and fairly comprehensive without boring the reader by being exhaustive. Well done." Also, a former MLB All-Star read it, and then gave it to his son, telling him, "Everything you need to know about baseball is in that book." Needless to say, these kind comments made my day.

Likewise, this booklet has a different approach to professional baseball. There are thousands of books about baseball out there—histories, biographies, statistical analyses, and "how to" books. There are also many interviews, and collections of interviews of past and present MLB players. These interviews usually focus on the player's biographies, or particular games, teams, or seasons. Sometimes, and to a lesser extent, the interviews focus on the players' personalities. That's all fine and dandy, and a lot of fans are interested in those aspects of baseball.

It occurred to me, however, that I had never seen or read an interview where the player or former player focused almost exclusively on how he went about doing his job. How did a player prepare in the off-season, and between games? What did he stress in training, and most importantly, how did he play his position? Did he do anything differently from how other ballplayers played his positon, and if so, what? I wanted to know all this, and realized that other baseball fans did too. That gave me the idea to do interviews of former MLB players, to sit down with them and find out how they did their jobs. Then, it occurred to me that I could put out a separate booklet for each interview, with a brief introduction for each player. That way, readers could pick and choose the specific baseball position that they wanted to read about.

After deciding on this project, I had the good fortune to get off to a flying start. I was talking about baseball with a long-time friend, Richard Redfearn, and he told me about Tom Brewer, a former Boston Red Sox All-Star pitcher. Tom was raised in a small town in South Carolina, and he moved back there after his professional baseball playing days were over. Richard is from an even smaller town just a few miles away, and he grew up listening on the radio as Tom pitched for the Red Sox. Richard put me in touch with Tom, and things fell into place after that. With that as background, let's get started.

# The Pitcher — Tom Brewer

Tom Brewer was a starting pitcher for the Boston Red Sox for eight seasons, from 1954 through 1961. Between starts, Tom was sometimes used in relief, and because he was the fastest runner on the Red Sox, he was also used as a pinch runner. Tom pitched against all the greats then in the American League, including Mickey Mantle, Al Kaline, Roger Maris, Larry Doby, and Yogi Berra. Tom also pitched against Ted Williams in spring training and Willie Mays in pre-season exhibition games.

During Tom's MLB pitching career, he had an overall winning record on a losing team; from 1954 through 1961, Tom went 91-70, while the Red Sox went 614-626. Tom's best year was 1956, when he went 19-9 on a team that went 84-70. That year, Tom's batting average was .298, and he was selected for the American League All-Star team.

After retiring from MLB in 1961—John F. Kennedy's first year in office—Tom returned to Cheraw, South Carolina, where he'd grown up. Tom worked as a probation officer for over a quarter-century, and is now retired. To this day, Tom lives in the pleasant and well-kept home he bought during his first year with the Red Sox organization. Over the past 54 years, Tom has freely given his time and energy to coaching pitching at his high school and to Cheraw youth. Tom's service has been recognized by his high school and community; Cheraw High School retired his uniform number, and named the school's baseball field in his honor. Back in the late 2000s, Tom Larwin wrote a very good biography of Tom Brewer, going into detail about his life and career, for the Society for American Baseball Research ("SABR"). You can find it easily by doing an internet search of "Tom Brewer and SABR."

When I interviewed Tom, I wanted something other than a recounting of his biography. I am fascinated by big league pitching, and I wanted Tom to tell me how he did what he did, including: how he trained in the off-season; how he prepared between starts; how he pitched to the great ballplayers I mentioned above; and what pitch he would start batters off with. I wanted to hear what it was like to pitch in Fenway Park, and whether he used the ballpark's peculiarities (such as the Green Monster out in left field) to his advantage.

I wrote Tom asking him if I could meet with him and he said yes, so in late April 2015, my wife Sandy and I sat down with Tom in his home just outside Cheraw. Although I'd been told that Tom was extremely nice, I really didn't know what to expect. Tom met us at his front door. He was tall and looked to be in good shape, had kegs for thighs, and really large hands. I found that everything I had heard about Tom was absolutely true. He was kind and hospitable—the epitome of what one would expect of a Southern gentleman. My family is from the South, so when Tom began to speak, the low rumble of his South Carolina drawl was comforting and familiar, and his words were clear, concise, and to the point.

We spent almost two hours talking with Tom about his career with the Red Sox, and I felt like a kid in a candy store. His descriptions and explanations, like his pitching (as you'll read), were focused and economical; he got right down to business. It was obvious that

Tom was smart, self-disciplined, comfortable in his own skin, and at peace with himself. It was also clear that Tom was proud to have played for the Red Sox for his entire MLB career.

I am deeply grateful to Tom for his kindness, generosity, and patience, and to his gracious wife Norma for putting up with me.

Now, I've set the stage. Here is the transcript of Tom's interview. Let's turn the page and see what Tom had to say about his craft.

# The Interview

**Q:** How often did you start?

**A:** Every four or five days. Mostly every five days, but I have started every four days. It took four days for me to get over that one day of pitching. The second day after I pitched I took batting practice and got ready to pitch for the next game.

**Q:** In terms of getting ready to pitch for the next game, what did you do? Did you have a routine?

**A:** Yes, I always had a routine. It was easy to get ready for the next game, because the main thing that I did was a lot of running. My legs were the most important thing for me as far as pitching was concerned. If you kept your legs in shape, you could keep your arm in shape. The day after I pitched, I would run 30 minutes. I would run sprints, I wouldn't jog. I would run sprints and I would run them just as hard as I could go.

**Q:** Would you run at the ballpark?

**A:** Yes, I ran at the ballpark while the rest of the team was taking batting practice. In spring training, the pitching coach ran all the pitchers together, and he'd throw balls to the pitchers to have them run after and catch. In my first year in the minors (the High Point-Thomasville Hi-Toms in the North Carolina State League), my manager would hit fly balls to us from foul line to foul line, which was tough. His name was Jim Gruzdis, and he was a heck of a manager. I liked him

11

very much. He was tough on us, but he was good to us.

**Q:** Did you throw any during the off-season?

**A:** No. I tried to rest my arm as much as possible, but I exercised it. I did weights in the basement. I have a basement in this house, and I set up a weight room down there, where I could work out the way that I wanted to. I didn't try to do curls. Curls are the worst thing in the world for a pitcher to do.

**Q:** What would you do?

**A:** I would do stretches, hanging weights on ropes and pulling (Tom raised his arm and brought it down by his side to show me the motion). You didn't want your arm to come up toward you with a curl. You need to stretch your arm downward and away. Otherwise your arm is going to be bent in a position that is coming up toward you. You can't do that time and time again without having elbow trouble.

**Q:** How often would you work out with weights?

**A:** Every day.

**Q:** Did you live here, in this house?

**A:** Yes.

**Q:** How long a period would you work out?

**A:** I'd work out for thirty to forty-five minutes.

**Q:** Would you run?

**A:** Oh yes.

**Q:** Where? Out here? (I pointed toward the state road that runs in front of Tom's house.)

**A:** There used to be a railroad track down the road about a half-mile away. I'd run to that railroad track and back every day. That was a mile a day, and I'd run, I wouldn't jog.

**Q:** When did you move into this house?

**A:** I moved into it the first year that I started playing with the Red Sox, which was 1954.

**Q:** When you came out of a game, did you use ice on your arm?

**A:** No. When you came out of that ball game, you were through until the next game. You didn't have any ice, you didn't put any heat, or anything like that on your arm. After we had pitched, we were through.

**Q:** I understand that you sometimes pitched in relief between starts. What did you do to get ready for that?

**A:** I'd go down to the bullpen, throw for about five minutes, and I was ready to go.

**Q:** Wow! Anything else that you can tell me about what you did between games?

**A:** Well, running was my main thing. A lot of players don't believe in it, but I do because I always thought my legs were the most important part of my pitching. My arm and my legs did the work—my shoulder, my arms, and my legs, those were the working parts. My lower back had to be strong too, so I did a lot of work keeping my back strong.

**Q:** What would you do to strengthen your back?

**A:** When I was downstairs in my weight room, I would take weights and do bending exercises with them, stretching my legs as I'd go down. A lot of people my

13

age can't stoop and then get up; I still can.

**Q:** Good for you! I hope you can still do it ten years from now.

**A:** (Chuckle) I hope so too!

**Q:** Do you still do some work with weights?

**A:** Yes.

**Q:** You look to be in shape. When you came to the door, I said to myself, "This guy is in good shape!"

**A:** I'm not going to get that far out of shape. Those boys up there at the high school, when I'm working with them, if they say "you can't run fast enough," or anything like that, I say "Get out there and let's go."

**Q:** (Laughing in appreciation) When you would pitch to a batter, and you pitched to him again during a game or during a series, would you remember how you'd pitched to him and what had worked?

**A:** I always tried to pitch them different. So, when I'd start off a game I'd pitch them one way, and in the middle of the game, I'd pitch to them backwards from what I'd started in the first part of the game. After I'd faced them twice, I would start backwards from what I'd done earlier. If I'd started them off with a fastball in the first part of the game, in the second part of the game I'd start them off with a breaking ball.

I never started a hitter off with a change-up. I didn't believe in throwing a change-up unless you threw him something hard to see to start with. Then you could throw a change-up and get him off-speed. If you threw him something easy to start with, all he was going to do was to sit up there and arm-swing and hit the ball. That's all he needed to do with a change-up. But, if you started him off with a fastball, he's got to be waiting on it. If you start him up with a fastball, and then throw a change-up, he's off-speed then. You've got to be thinking about how he's looking at you and how he's going to look at it. For example, if you threw him two fastballs in a row, and then you threw him a breaking ball, you may be thinking, "he's looking for a fastball." I didn't do that. I'd throw as many as three or four breaking balls in a row.

**Q:** When you say "a breaking ball," you're talking about a curve?

**A:** A curve ball, yeah. I did not throw a slider.

**Q:** Did they have sliders then?

**A:** Yes.

**Q:** So, all the pitches that I had in my book, people threw them back then?

**A:** Yes. Mel Parnell (Boston Red Sox pitcher) had the best slider that I can remember. He had a good curveball, but his slider was his best pitch.

**Q:** And your best pitch?

**A:** Was a curveball.

**Q:** Would you start them with a curveball?

**A:** I have, yeah.

**Q:** Can you recall the longest at-bat that a hitter ever had with you?

**A:** That would come with hitters like Nelson Fox (White Sox) and Harvey Kuenn (with the Tigers and Indians during Tom's career), hitters like that...hitters that didn't strike out much. They were what I call "Punch and Judy Hitters" (a hitter who hits with little power). They couldn't generally hit the long ball, but every once in a while they'd hit the long ball on you. But if you kept it off-speed on them, they'd foul it off. They'd foul off a good off-speed pitch. You had to keep them guessing—you had keep them guessing more than you were guessing, and you had to keep pitching that way.

**Q:** Did you find that pitching against pitchers was tougher?

**A:** No. Pitchers always wanted to hit against pitchers, because they're trying to show that they can hit against you just as good as you can hit against them.

**Q:** That's kind of what I thought…that it would be more fun.

**A:** Oh yeah. It's more fun to hit against the pitcher.

**Q:** What was the hardest out that you ever had to get?

**A:** Nelson Fox.

**Q:** Can you tell me about it?

**A:** Well, he fouled off about twenty pitches. (Tom laughs) He was a good little hitter.

Everybody thinks that the sluggers are hard to pitch to. They're really the easiest to pitch to. They had a weakness. Every slugger had a weakness.

**Q:** Same weakness or different?

**A:** No. Every one of them was different. They had a blind spot, and you had to find it. Mickey Mantle had a blind spot, a little bit above the waist. If you threw a fastball up there, he couldn't hit it. It's location.

**Q:** Aside from yourself, who was the best pitcher you ever saw?

**A:** Herb Score. He played for Cleveland. He threw the hardest ball I saw. He threw it a hundred and something miles an hour back then. The only hitter who could hit him consistently was Ted Williams. Ted Williams said "Nobody alive can throw the ball by me." And he was right.

**Q:** Did you ever pitch to Ted?

**A:** Oh, I pitched batting practice against him.

**Q:** How'd you do?

**A:** He didn't like to hit against me. He said I broke too many bats for him.

**Q:** Did you throw high and inside?

**A**: Well, no. I threw a "heavy ball," and it would move all the time, and hit him on the fist and break his bat.

(A heavy ball is a ball that breaks late, and according to what I found when I looked it up, it would put a shock through a bat, and hurt a catcher's hand. One commentator said that, "Getting jammed on a heavy ball feels like you just hit a brick.")

I broke five bats for him at batting practice one day. Things like that you don't see because that happens in spring training. After that, he never would hit against me in spring training. He said, "I'm up there to hit," and I said, "It doesn't do me any good to throw you a ball and say 'Here it is.' I'm out here to work on my pitching. If I'm out here on this mound, I'm working on my pitching the same as you're working on your hitting. I can't do me any good just throwing you easy pitches up there to hit. I could do it, but it's not doing me any good."

**Q:** He was older, wasn't he? He'd been up since 1939, right?

**A:** Oh yeah. He'd just gotten back from his second tour of duty, serving in Korea, and he was something else.

What we always fussed at him about was that he would always help the hitters from the opposing teams who were having slumps. They'd come to him for help, and he would help them.

**Q:** That's just wrong.

**A:** Well I think it was too. But he said, "As long as they come to me for help, I'm going to help them." That was the way he was.

Ted and I were friends. I told him after I broke three or four bats for him in spring training batting practice, "By golly, if I'd had you to pitch against, I'd have won 30 games." He laughed and said, "I'd hit you every time I'd go out there," and I said, "Yes, and I'd break that many bats for you too." I made friends with Ted to start with, and when we got on planes to go different places, Ted and I sat next to one another.

**Q:** Who was the best batter you ever <u>saw</u>?

**A:** The best all-around batter was Kaline. [Al Kaline, Detroit Tigers]

**Q:** The best batter you ever <u>faced</u>?

**A:** Kaline.

**Q:** I understand Yogi Berra was a good bad-ball hitter.

**A:** Yogi Berra, you don't throw any bad pitches to him.

**Q:** Why?

**A:** He hits it.

**Q:** How about if you threw him a good pitch?

**A:** If you threw a good pitch you had a better chance of getting him out than if you threw a bad pitch.

**Q:** Why is that? Is that just the way it was?

**A:** That's just the way it was. I threw him a slow curve that was that high (Tom holds out his hand about five or six inches from the floor.). He hit it out of the ballpark. That was just one of those pitches; I'd never thrown him one before. It was that high off the ground, and he "golfed" it out of the ballpark. That was at Yankee Stadium. He hit it right around the pole out in right field, where it's short.

**Q:** That leads me right into my next question. When you pitched in Fenway, did you use the park's features, such as the Green Monster out in left field?

**A:** You know, everybody fought the Green Monster. I used it to my advantage. If you had a good hard ball off the wall, and if you've got the fielders who know how to play that wall, it was a single. In other places, it was a double. You had a lot of people saying, "I hate that wall." But I thought it was to my advantage to let them hit the wall, and the ball would come back to the fielders. If a runner was on second base, and the batter hit the ball hard off the wall, he didn't score from second base.

**Q:** Would you slow down as the game went along and you became tired? Would you throw more off-speed stuff?

**A:** No. I bore down. I didn't throw more off-speed pitches. I threw the pitches that I knew I could get people out with.

**Q:** If you saw a rookie come up, and you hadn't faced him before, first time up to the Show, how would you start him off?

**A:** We knew when they came up what they could hit and what they couldn't hit. We had good sources of information for everybody who came up. In fact, they would be at spring training, and a lot of times we pitched against them at spring training. But if we hadn't seen them, and they came up in the middle of the year, we had scouts who had scouted them when they were playing down. They gave us the information about what they could hit and what they couldn't hit. They gave us the feedback from the minor leagues up to the big leagues, so we knew about what everybody was doing. We weren't left in the blind all the time. You think everybody was hitting and pitching in the blind, but we weren't.

**Q:** If pitchers came up that you hadn't seen before, did you have information on them for when you were batting?

**A:** Oh yeah.

**Q:** The reason I asked is because from what I've read, you not only were one heck of a pitcher, but you could hit, and hit for power, and you could run. I was reading about your pinch running. You could do that because you worked your legs?

**A:** Yeah. I liked to run, and I could run pretty good. We had players on our ball club, pitchers and all, who thought they were fast. They couldn't outrun me. I pinch ran a lot. Did you read about that too? (Tom chuckled)

**Q:** Yeah, I did.

**A:** Well everybody who came up, the new rookies and everyone else said, "Well, we got to try the fastest man on the team." We'd run sprints, and everybody would try to keep up with me and they couldn't do it.

**Q:** So, you could throw a fastball, a curve ball, and off-speed (different types), correct?

**A:** Yes.

**Q:** Did you have a favorite catcher?

**A:** Yes. Sammy White was my favorite catcher. We could pitch a whole ballgame, and he never called a signal.

**Q:** He knew what you were going to throw?

**A:** He said, "You just throw what you want to and I'll catch it."

**Q:** Not a lot of wild pitches?

**A:** Not a lot of wild pitches.

**Q:** How was your (overall) control?

**A:** Erratic. I had some days that I'd have good control, the next day it would be a little worse, and then the next day it would come back and I'd pitch good. But, it wasn't as good as it should have been.

**Q:** Did you have a good pitching coach up there (with the Red Sox)?

**A:** Well, yes I did. "Boo" (Dave) Ferris was my pitching coach, and if he found something wrong that you were doing, he'd correct you. He never said much to me.

I wish I had had a pitching coach who had told me a little bit of what I'm teaching now to these kids who don't have good control, because there is a way can throw the ball so that you can throw strikes every time you throw, if you throw it that way. And I'm teaching these kids in high school how to do that, and some of them who couldn't even find the plate can find the plate now, where it's easy for them. If I'd had that same kind of teaching when I was in the major leagues, I would have had better control.

**Q:** Do you watch their mechanics?

**A:** Yes.

**Q:** And tell them about their legs and that they need to run?

**A:** Yes. The mechanics are real good if you know what you're talking about. Every pitch that you throw, there are about nine ways that you can throw that one pitch. It's that way with a fastball, and the same way with a curveball. And there are so many different ways you can throw a breaking ball that the ball will break differently. You want the ball to go down on a breaking ball. Most pitchers want it to go sideways.

A fellow would say, "My curve ball breaks this way," (Tom moves his hand from side to side) and I'd say "Well, that's not a very good 'out' pitch." He'd say "Why?" I'd say, "Think about how the bat's swung. It's swung the same way (side to side). You throw a breaking ball that way (sideways) it's on the same plane as the bat." I want it going down so that you've got about that much space (Tom held his hands one above the other, so that they were only two or three inches apart) to hit that ball.

**Q:** Did you know when you went out to the mound from warming up whether or not your control was there?

**A:** I knew when I went out there what kind of control I was going to have, from loosening up.

**Q:** Did you ever go out there thinking you were going to have a good day, and then had a bad day?

**A:** Yes.

**Q:** What happened?

**A:** I didn't have a good fastball. After loosening up, I'd go out to the mound thinking I had the best stuff in the world, and I'd go out there and think I couldn't break a pane of glass. And that day, I'd usually pitch the best ballgame I had. It's because you concentrated so much more on what you were doing, and you'd hit spots so much easier.

**Q:** Because you're thinking about it?

**A:** That's right. Because you know you don't have the good stuff that day. So you pitch, and you have better control, and you throw more strikes, and the curve ball may not look like it's breaking, but it's usually breaking better than you think.

**Q:** Did you ever go out to the mound and have concentration issues?

**A:** I'd go out there lots of times and have concentration problems.

**Q:** Thinking about other stuff going on?

**A:** Sometimes that, or sometimes something was going on at home with my parents, and the next thing you know you're thinking "I should be there, with my mother and father."

**Q:** People would come from down here (Cheraw) to watch you play at Fenway. Could you spot them when you were out there on the mound?

**A:** Sometimes I didn't even know they were there.

**Q:** But were you ever able to see them?

**A:** Oh yeah. I knew where they were because I got them the tickets. You know, the funny thing about that is that people coming to the game wanted me to know they were there, but when they got in the stands I never even thought about them. I tried to think of nothing but what I was doing out there on the mound, between me and the catcher.

**Q:** Did you have any tricks you would use when it was one of those days you were trying not to think about what was going on with your family?

**A:** I tried to do that a lot of times. If you ever saw me turn around and look at center field for about two or three minutes, then I was trying to get my mind back on what I was supposed to be doing. That's the best way you can do it, is just to turn around, blank your mind while you're turned around, and just stand there. I've had umpires come out there and ask me, "What's wrong? It's time to go to work." I said, "Okay, I'm ready."

But you do that intentionally so that you can get your mind back together, and it also makes the hitter worry about what you're going to do.

**Q:** He thinks you're thinking about him, and...

**A:** I'm not worried about the hitter, I'm worried about what I'm thinking about.

**Q:** Did you ever think about getting hit by a comebacker when you're out there?

**A:** I never thought about it. I had one hit back so hard at me one time that it went between my hat and my head as I went down.

**Q:** Did you ever get hit by a comebacker?

**A:** Oh yeah.

**Q:** Where?

**A:** On the knee.

**Q:** Did they take you out for the rest of the game?

**A:** No.

I also caught a line drive with my bare hand, and broke two bones in my hand. Gus Triandos hit the ball. He was about 6'6", and weighed about 260 at that time. He hit a line drive back and I caught it with my bare hand.

**Q:** What was his name?

**A:** Gus Triandos. He caught for the Orioles back then.

**Q:** Big target?

**A:** Yeah. But you know I didn't like a big target. The little guys who get down low are who I liked to pitch to.

**Q:** Because they made you focus?

**A:** Oh yes.

**Q:** I'd think that they would be a lot harder.

**A:** Well they were, but it made you concentrate more. The big guys stood up, and it made you pitch high. I wanted to pitch low because I throw a sinking fastball. Everybody says, "When you get two strikes, you want to throw a high fastball." I never wanted to throw that. I think that's a waste of pitching to throw a high fastball when you have two strikes. I think it's a waste of pitching and a waste of time. A hitter's got a weakness. If you've got an extra pitch to throw, throw it at that weakness, if anything.

**Q:** When you're up there on the mound, and you've just got a big league power hitter out, do you have any time to feel anything, or are you thinking about the next batter?

**A:** I don't even think about it.

**Q:** Do you think about it later, after you get out of the game?

**A:** I never think about anything when I'm on that mound but throwing, pitching. I know what I want to do, and I'm thinking about what I want to do if I have balls hit back to me, and I know what I want to do if I have to cover a base; and if I have to cover a base, I know where I've got to go.

Pitchers nowadays don't know how to cover first base. If you watch a pitcher nowadays, from the mound they go straight to the base. That's wrong.

**Q:** You go behind the base, don't you?

**A:** No, you go straight to the line, and then you go down, because that way you don't have to look at the base, or look for the base. You go about five yards down to the line, then you go to the bag. You don't even have to look for the bag because you just run and you'll touch the bag. Most of the pitchers have to look for the bag when they go straight to it.

**Q:** After the game, and you've won, do you feel good?

**A:** Oh yeah.

**Q:** Do you go over the game in your mind?

**A:** Well, I go over the game after I get home. While I'm at the ballpark, I don't think about anything but just getting a shower and cooling off.

**Q:** After a game, does it take you a while to rest, to go to sleep?

**A:** Takes me a while to go to sleep. I'm so hyped up then it just takes me a while to do. I can go to a ballgame and really get whopped, pitchers hitting on me and batters hitting on me, and I'll get home and it'll worry me and I'll think about that whole thing all night long.

**Q:** You see it all over again?

**A:** Oh yeah, and I say "Why did this happen?" But after I get through analyzing everything, it wasn't anything but that I was making bad pitches. When you make bad pitches, it costs you. A pitcher nowadays, if he makes three mistakes in a ballgame, and he gets by with them, he'll win a ballgame. That's the most mistakes he can make and get by with it. (By the way, Tom watches a lot of MLB games. When we arrived, Tom was watching the Braves play the Blue Jays on a large flat panel television in his living room. The game stayed on, in the background and with the sound muted, while we were visiting, although we didn't pay any attention to it once we started talking.)

**Q:** When you mention pitchers' mistakes, what do you mean?

**A:** When I say "making mistakes," I mean that they throw pitches in the wrong place for a hitter to hit. See, we'd go over every hitter before the ballgame, and we'd tell the rest of the players how we were going to pitch a certain hitter. When you make a mistake and they hit a home run or something, then YOU made the mistake.

**Q:** You guessed wrong?

**A:** We didn't guess. We made a mistake about where

we placed our arm to throw that pitch. See, every pitch-er has a place that they make their arm go for a differ-ent pitch.

**Q:** You didn't have film back then, so you couldn't re-ally watch yourself?

**A:** No. But a pitcher nowadays, if he'll throw over-hand and come down by his left knee (for a right-hand-ed pitcher), he'll throw strikes. Now, if he throws and he comes out here and he goes across here (Tom start-ed his hand moving from an angle off to the side of his head, and then moved his hand across his body), he's only got about that much space (roughly six inches) to throw strikes. Now you think about it, if the pitcher throws overhand and comes down by his left knee, he's got this much of a strike zone (Tom holds his hands about two feet apart). If you watch the pitchers when they're warming up, and they pitch like this (bringing their arms across their bodies), you wonder how they're going to throw strikes. But they've pitched that way so much, and he's got to know where his release is.

The release point for a pitcher is very important. For most pitchers, when they are throwing sidearm, their release point is going to be right along in here (Tom arm is extended, and his hand is stopped at a point away from his body). That's going to be outside. If they start it here (throwing overhand), it's going to be inside, but what they are doing is getting that hitter to adjust to that pitch. By starting from up here (overhand), the pitcher is giving that hitter a far larger strike zone to worry about.

Also, if you throw a curveball, and you come over-hand, which way is it going to go? It's going to go down.

**Q:** Which is what you want?

**A:** That's right. You want it to go down. Any time a pitcher throws a slider or a curveball and it goes sideways, it's not as good a pitch as the one that goes down. You throw the ball sideways, and it's on the same line with the bat. The hitter knows that when you pitch to him. He's watched you pitch enough to know what your weaknesses are too. So, you've got to give him something to look at. I know I've thrown sidearm curveballs before and got hit, but I didn't throw many of them because all I was trying to do was to give the hitter a different pitch to look at.

**Q:** Would you practice it much that day before the game?

**A:** No. I wouldn't show it to them when I was warming up. I might throw a sidearm fastball, but if I did I made sure I got it outside. I wouldn't throw it inside because you can hit a guy every time he throws a sidearm fastball.

**Q:** During a rain delay, how would you stay loosened up?

**A:** I wouldn't. I'd sit there, and then come out and get loosened up when the game re-started. They gave you plenty of time.

**Q:** How many pitches would you get to throw then?

**A:** Well, a lot of pitchers take more time than they need...I'd say a majority of them do. They aren't doing a thing but tiring themselves out. I think you need to go out there and throw, maybe 25-50 pitches, and you ought to be ready to go by then.

**Q:** When you were out there on the mound, did you ever feel your back tightening up?

**A:** That's the worst thing that there is. If your back stiffens up, and you can go back in and get it loosened up before you go back out to the mound, it's easy. But most of the time, you don't have time to go get yourself a trainer to loosen your back up. So, a lot of times I'd hang from the roof of the dugout; I'd hang down and just pull the back muscles loose, and you can throw with no problem at all then.

**Q:** What's the longest game you ever threw?

**A:** Fourteen innings.

**Q:** Whew! Did you win it?

**A:** Yes. I was also in a sixteen inning game. I didn't finish, but we won the ballgame.

**Q:** Did you pitch often at night?

**A:** Most of the time I pitched all the night games.

If we pitched a double-header (and we had more double-headers back then than they do now—and I don't know why we don't have more double-headers now than we do), and we had a day-night double-header, well most of the time Frank Sullivan pitched the day game and I pitched the night game.

**Q:** Did you like pitching at night?

**A:** It didn't bother me. I'd rather have pitched the day game, but they said "You pitch the night game."

**Q:** Why?

**A:** I don't know.

**Q:** Why would you rather have pitched the day game?

**A:** I had no reason to dislike pitching at night, but it was just my theory that I'd rather pitch during the daylight.

**Q:** Back when you were pitching, they didn't black out centerfield, did they?

**A:** No.

**Q:** So, you had to deal with the crowd out there?

**A:** Yeah.

**Q:** Did you throw from the windup or from the stretch?

**A:** I threw from the stretch.

**Q:** You didn't change up because somebody was on base?

**A:** No.

**Q:** Did you throw from the stretch because you felt better because it gave you better rhythm?

**A:** Well, your control is better if you come right down to it. I threw from the windup too, but I threw from the stretch and I had better control of it. That's the reason why they used me more in relief; because I could pitch easier from the stretch.

You have to think about your leg position. If you kick your leg up high to throw from the stretch, you're giving that baserunner two or three seconds to run on you. But, if you take it from here (Tom slid his front leg forward, as if coming off the mound for a pitch), you don't give him that much time. That's why I teach my kids to slide their legs apart. Don't lift your leg up, because if you do you're going to give that baserunner two to three seconds, that's going to cost you a steal, and you're going to get the man in scoring position.

**Q:** Did you have a good pick-off move?

**A:** Well, you have to practice that.

**Q:** You got better?

**A:** (Tom laughs)

**Q:** Did your fastball slow down over time?

**A:** I think it did over time. I think it slowed down because of age.

**Q:** They didn't have radar guns back then?

**A:** No.

**Q:** Toward the end of the season, after the All-Star break, did all that travel start to wear you down?

**A:** Oh yeah. Every time you traveled, and you'd go off and spend the night in a hotel, you got tired. That is a tiresome thing, to have to spend the night in a hotel. You have to go out to eat, so sometimes after a night game it would be midnight before you got to the hotel, then you have to eat, so sometimes it's 2:00 a.m. before you get to bed. So you figure it out.

**Q:** Not only that, it's constant, and the beds aren't comfortable, and...

**A:** The thing of it is, they gave us good rooms. We had exceptional hotels where we stayed. I'll have to agree with the club for doing it that way. They gave us the best rooms they could get, and some of us had suites we stayed in.

**Q:** That's pretty good.

**A:** Yep. Well, if we had a night game tonight, and you were pitching tomorrow, a lot of times the manager would tell you to go on home, or back to the hotel. He gave us that little extra time to rest. So that was good. But, he didn't always do that. He didn't do that for me because he said, "You might have to run." Those are the times you'd say, "Well, you're not being fair to me as far as my pitching is concerned. I like to rest as much as the rest of them." But it wasn't going to keep me from winning though, because I was going to go out and give my best.

**Q:** Now, did any pitcher throw a pitch that wasn't like any other that you'd ever seen before?

**A:** No.

**Q:** Earlier you said that Mantle had a weakness. Did Maris have a weakness?

**A:** He had a weakness, but it wasn't as easy to pitch to as Mantle's was.

**Q:** What was it?

**A:** It was a little low and inside. When you threw it low and inside, he was going to foul it. If you threw it a little bit quicker he wouldn't hit it. But the regular pitchers would throw it in there, and he'd hit a lot of home runs that way. Because they were trying to hit that spot, and they weren't quick enough, and he could hit it out.

**Q:** Mantle, Maris, or Berra—which one was the toughest out?

**A:** Berra.

**Q:** In preseason, did you ever face Willie Mays?

**A:** Yes.

**Q:** How was he?

**A:** The last pitch I pitched to him he hit a home run. (Tom smiles.) That was in spring training in Arizona. I hated Arizona.

**Q:** Why's that?

**A:** You'd get hot, and as soon as you sat down in the dugout and before you could go back out, you were dry.

**Q:** (Sandy) It's too hot there.

**A:** It's 100 degrees out there, and while you were pitching you'd warm up good, but as soon as you walked in that dugout, and before they could get three outs, you'd be completely dry.

**Q:** Sandy hates the Arizona heat!

**A:** Well, I never liked it.

**Q:** Did you ever face Jackie Robinson?

**A:** No, I never faced Jackie.

But I faced his counterpart in the American League, Larry Doby.

**Q:** How was he to pitch to?

**A:** Larry was a good player...a real good player. And he was a good hitter. Whenever you pitched to him in tight situations, when his team needed runs, he really bore down. When men were on base, he was really a conscientious player, because he wanted to do what was right for the club.

I didn't face Jackie, but I did pitch five scoreless innings against the Dodgers in Miami, the first year I went to spring training with the Red Sox (1954). I pitched 29 scoreless innings in spring training that year.

**Q:** That's amazing!

I'm going to stop for a second. You know, it seems to me that the Dodgers and all the other teams today are spending all this money on position players, but the

Giants figured it out. You can pretty much have average fielding and hitting, but it's all about pitching. That's where you put your money.

**A:** That's right. Some of their pitchers though have been there for a long time, and they're beginning to get some age on them and they're slowing down, and they still think they can pitch the same as when they were 21 or 22 years old. They can't do it. They've got to change their style a little bit. They can still win, but they've got to change their style to be able to pitch. When you get a little bit of age on you, you've got to change, I don't care how much it is, but you've got to change a lot as you go along. Every year you've got to change some, I don't care if it's just a little bit, but you've got to change some.

**Q:** Otherwise they've got you figured out, plus you're slowing down?

**A:** That's right.

**Q:** You know who I liked watching pitch? Greg Maddux.

**A:** I loved to watch him pitch. If you watched him pitch, it's just what I told you. He's up here (Tom holds his right arm straight up), and then down by that leg. He had the best control of any pitcher I ever saw. He could take that ball, and turn that wrist just a little bit, and that ball would move just a little bit, and that's all he had to do.

But it's amazing that the pitchers don't work on making the ball move. I always told pitchers that I taught, "You've got to make the ball move." It only takes a little thing. The most important part of pitching is what? That right there (Tom holds up his hand and wiggles his thumb).

**Q:** The thumb?

**A:** That thumb. That's the most important part. You grab the baseball and you put your thumb on the seam, all you've got to do is take that and do that (Tom twists his thumb slightly) while you throw it.

**Q:** What do you think of today's pitchers as opposed to the pitchers when you pitched in terms of durability, training, and pitch count?

**A:** I don't think they're in shape. I don't think any pitcher today is in shape. I don't think they get in shape. Now they might tell you that they're in shape, but I don't believe it.

**Q:** (Sandy) Because?

**A:** Because I don't think they do enough work between their pitching starts.

**Q:** Which reminds me, did you throw fast—meaning not a lot of time between pitches?

**A:** I pitched a couple of ball games, even back then, in an hour and a half.

**Q:** Whoa!

**A:** If they had let me, I would have pitched in less time than that, because when I got the ball, I was ready to throw it.

**Q:** You didn't want to be thinking?

**A:** I didn't need to think. When I'm out there, I've already got my mind made up what I'm doing. Every pitcher out there should already have his mind made up when that hitter comes to the plate what he's going to throw him and how he's going to pitch him.

**Q:** You don't have to think?

**A:** I don't have to think, because I already know what that hitter can hit, and what he can't hit. All I've got to do is get the ball and do it. But these pitchers today, they go out there and kill too much time.

**Q:** So, durability, they're not in shape? Training, they don't train hard enough?

**A:** I don't think they're in shape. I don't think the pitching coaches and the clubs require them to get in shape. They pitch five innings, and that's all they require of them.

I don't believe the pitchers do enough running. I don't think they do enough running to stay in shape year-round. If you watch a pitcher whenever they hit it and get on base, they're breathing hard. Every pitcher that you watch—and some of the position players are that way too—they're not getting enough running in to keep them from breathing so hard when they get on base. You take a player and he gets on base, and they ask him to steal second base, and he's breathing just as hard as he can. That tells me that he's not in shape, because if he runs from home to first and second, he ought not to be breathing hard at all. I think being in good condition would extend the longevity of a player.

**Q:** Five innings is crazy. They're getting $20 million a year to pitch five-inning games.

**A:** You can say what you want, but any time you're paying a pitcher a million dollars to pitch five innings, you're getting cheated.

**Q:** Yeah, you are. Pitch count; do you think that's important?

**A:** No. I've thrown 200 pitches in a ball game. It didn't bother me.

**Q:** And you were ready to go again at the next rotation?

**A:** Yes.

**Q:** And you could have thrown in relief (between starts)?

**A:** Yes. What makes you mad though is that you see pitchers go out there and not even run out a ball that's been hit on the ground. They don't run out fly balls. They don't run out foul balls. They don't do anything that they're supposed to do to make the game look interesting. They're killing the ballgame by not hustling. They're paid millions of dollars, and they don't hustle. They don't earn their money.

**Q:** Do you think that it made a difference in how long a pitcher could go when MLB lowered the mound ten inches after the 1968 season?

**A:** No, I don't think it made a difference in how long he could go. I think it made a difference in how hard he threw, because pushing off the rubber with that extra height gave him a little extra speed. They slowed a lot of pitchers down when they lowered that mound. If it had stayed up like it had been, you were throwing downhill all the time. When they flattened the mound, you couldn't throw as hard.

**Q:** So, if they can't throw as hard, the pitchers would still be trying to throw hard, and they'd use up too much energy?

**A:** It would have an effect on how long the pitcher could go, because he was trying to still throw as hard as he could when it was high.

**Q:** And there's no reason to throw that hard?

**A:** No.

**Q:** So they still ought to be able to go out there and pitch a full game?

**A:** Right.

**Q:** Thinking about it, you've been coaching pitching for over fifty years, and you watched the mound go down at the high school level?

**A:** Oh yeah.

**Q:** So, what you just told me is what you saw?

**A:** Oh yeah. When you're coaching, the main thing you try to teach a kid is to be smooth with his delivery. If he's smooth with his delivery, he can throw strikes. If he's herky-jerky, he's not going to throw strikes. A lot of times a kid will get about halfway through his windup, and he jumps at the plate.

If you watch a pitcher—even in the major leagues— he'll start jumping at the plate, and he can't throw strikes when he does that all the time. But if he's smooth with it, he can throw strikes nine times out of ten.

Also, a pitcher shouldn't rush his pitches. If he slows down he can throw strikes.

**Q:** Let's talk about hitting for a bit.

**A:** I loved to hit. I always thought that I could hit as good as some of the infielders did out there. In fact, when I was playing my first year in pro ball (1954), our third baseman got hurt, and the manager put me in to play third base for about five games. Boston found out about it, and called up and told him to get me out of there because I might get hurt. I don't get hurt easily, because I played the game like it ought to be played. I played hard, and I played it like it's supposed to be. I was in shape when I played, I didn't care how it came around—I've been hit in the stomach with the ball, I've been hit in the chest with the ball, and I've been hit on each shoulder with the ball, but it didn't bother me.

**Q:** Because you were in shape?

**A:** I was in shape. If you get in shape, I don't care where the ball hits you, you're going to stay alright. But these guys who get hit in the leg with a line drive coming back, they're going to have to go out of the ballgame because they're not in shape. If they get hit in the leg, and they've run enough, those legs can take that.

**Q:** They didn't have helmets when you played. Do you think the game is better or worse with helmets?

**A:** I think they made the game safer.

**Q:** But now they're trying to make pitchers wear helmets. Have you seen some of the things they want those boys to wear? They're not going to wear them.

**A:** No. If a pitcher is doing his job, and he pitches like he's supposed to, he shouldn't have to worry about getting hurt. Most pitchers throw the ball, and they've got their back turned toward the hitter after they release the ball. If you watch them when they throw the ball, they're off-balance. They're trying to throw the ball so hard that their arms are wrapped around and their backs are to the plate, and they leave their heads open, their backs open, and their legs open. So they've got a chance of being hurt; they don't realize it but they do.

If a pitcher is pitching like he's supposed to, he should be in this position right here (Tom stands as if he's just finished his pitch and is at the base at the front of the mound, holding his glove hand in front of

him, high up at the top of his chest, waiting for anything that may be coming back at him.). If they teach it
that way, and the pitcher is in this position right here,
he shouldn't have to worry about getting hurt. He can
see the ball coming, and he's got the glove right here
(Tom glances down at his glove hand) to protect himself.
I just don't think a helmet is going to be the right answer. I think the answer is to be in the right position to
be able to field the ball when it's hit back at you.

**Q:** He can put it right up over his face?

**A:** Maddux always had it the right way; he had his
glove right here.

**Q:** I'll have to go back and watch Maddux.

**A:** You watch Maddux, you'll find out that his glove is
right here (Tom again raises his glove hand and looks at
it). He was the best fielding pitcher that I saw. Bobby
Shantz was another one. He had his glove right there
too. He was the best fielding pitcher in Yankee Stadium. He was real good. He was small but he was
quick. He won a Gold Glove about four or five years in a
row. I didn't stand a chance as long as he was with the
Yankees. (Shantz pitched for the Yankees from 1957
to 1960. He won eight consecutive Gold Glove Awards
from 1957 to 1964.)

**Q:** Would the manager generally let you hit, or would
he often put on a bunt if there was a runner on first
base?

**A:** Well, mine would let me hit as long as I didn't have
to move anybody over. But, I didn't mind bunting, because I could bunt and get the ball over and beat it out.

**Q:** Did you use a light bat or a heavy bat?

41

**A:** Medium.

**Q:** Any particular reason?

**A:** Just felt good.

**Q:** I read too that you had an extremely fast move toward first base, and for a right-hander, that's pretty darned good.

**A:** Well, I worked on it.

A lot of people didn't work on having balls hit back at them either. I did. In spring training, I would throw the ball or make like I was throwing the ball, and I'd have the coaches hit the ball back through the box at me. I did that because for my protection, I needed it. I told them, "Don't hit it easy, hit it hard." You had to have them hit it hard in order to protect yourself.

**Q:** So then you'd be ready when the season started, so that if there was a ball that came right back at you, you'd be able to save yourself.

**A:** That's right.

**Q:** So, when you came off the mound, your glove was up and ready?

**A:** Yes.

**Q:** Between starts, did you take batting practice every day?

**A:** At home we did. All of the pitchers took batting practice at home.

**Q:** What's your thinking about the designated hitter?

**A:** I don't like it. I think the game was made for nine players to play the game, and not for somebody to substitute for them.

**Q:** I totally agree.

**A:** I think it should be where the pitchers have to hit, and win or lose, that's the way it should be played.

**Q:** (Sandy) Why do they use a designated hitter?

**A:** The American League wanted to see more hits, more home runs, and more runs scored. That's the object of the designated hitter. I think it's wrong. And some pitchers can hit. And some of them are not given the opportunity to hit, but they should be. I know for a fact that I could hit better than some of my players who were playing every day. I hit .298 in 1956, and I had two home runs that year. I could have hit a lot better than that if I'd had the batting practice that the position players had.

**Q:** What was your best pitch to hit?

**A:** Curveball.

**Q:** Because you were a pitcher, could you figure out what they were going to throw to you?

**A:** I knew what they were going to throw to me. I knew that if I swung at a fastball, the next two pitches were going to be breaking balls. I learned to hit the curve ball, so if they threw me curve balls, I could hit them. Every pitcher that tried to get me out would either throw me a slider or a curveball.

**Q:** And you'd be ready for it?

**A:** That's right. I didn't look for a fastball; I looked for a breaking ball.

**Q:** So if a fastball came, you'd let it go by?

**A:** That's right. Or, I'd hit it to right field. I wouldn't try to pull it. The home runs I hit, I hit to left field; and

I hit one to dead-centerfield. I hit one in Chicago that hit the 415 sign. I hit that against Billy Pierce (White Sox pitcher, and seven-time All-Star).

**Q:** Who was the best pitcher you ever hit against?

**A:** I'd say Herb Score. (As noted above, Score pitched for the Cleveland Indians.)

**Q:** Did you ever hit against Don Larson?

**A:** Yeah.

**Q:** Was he good?

**A:** He was good.

**Q:** Why do they always make out like he was a journey-man pitcher?

**A:** Well, he was a good pitcher. He knew how to pitch to hitters. He was a good hitter himself, and he knew how to pitch to them. He could hit the long ball too. (Larson was a good enough hitter that, during his career, he was used as a pinch hitter 66 times.)

There is a way that you pitch to hitters, and a way that you pitch to batters that can't hit. A lot of people who can't hit, you just say, "Well, here it is, hit it," but you've got good enough stuff so that you can throw it by them. But a hitter, you can't throw it by him.

**Q:** So if they started you out with a fastball, you'd take it. Did they always start you out with a fastball?

**A:** Not always.

**Q:** If they started you out with a curve, were you quick enough to be able to see it and hit it?

**A:** Oh yeah, I could see it coming out of the hand.

**Q:** So you didn't always take a first pitch?

**A:** If it was where I wanted, I hit it. I didn't take all fastballs. If there were ones where I wanted it, I'd hit it.

**Q:** Whitey Ford – did you hit against him?

**A:** Yeah. I pitched a lot of games against Whitey.

**Q:** So if you were up there on the mound, and you retaliated against somebody, either because they were stealing your signs, or the guy showed you up or something, would they retaliate against you personally, or someone on your team?

**A:** Usually against me.

**Q:** Did you get hit a lot?

**A:** No. I was too quick for them.

**Q:** (Sandy) They tried but you were able to get out of the way?

**A:** I could usually tell when a pitcher was going to try to hit me.

**Q:** How?

**A:** Because, when he got to pitching, and some of the good hitters came up and he wouldn't throw at them. And then you came up there, and the catcher is back there saying, "Well, he's going to get you today." I said "No he ain't, but if he does, I'm going to get him." I'd tell him flat out, "If he throws at me, he's going to get decked too."

**Q:** And that's what you'd do?

**A:** That's right.

**Q:** Next time up?

**A:** That's right. Because you see, back when I was pitching, you could throw at someone, and the umpires wouldn't warn you or anything.

**Q:** That's just part of the game?

**A:** Just part of the game. And I think it should be that way now.

**Q:** So, you would throw at someone intentionally?

**A:** Yes.

**Q:** To hit them in the back or below the waist?

**A:** Yes.

**Q:** Would you throw at their head?

**A:** Yes. (Tom pauses for a moment, cocks his head slightly to the side, and smiles.) You know, if you're going to be a good pitcher, you've got to be a little mean.

**Q:** Do you think a baserunner coming into home from third base ought to be able to slam into the catcher?

**A:** No. But the catcher shouldn't be able to block the plate like they used to. They'd get in front of the plate about that far (Tom holds his hands up about a foot apart), and block the plate; I think that's wrong. I think they can sit on the plate, and that would be fine, but not that far in front of the plate.

**Q:** If they're sitting on the plate, do you think they are fair game?

**A:** I think they're fair game. But, if you take the catchers who got hurt, they were sitting that far (again, Tom holds his hands up and apart) in front of the plate.

**Q:** Did you steal bases much?

**A:** Yes.

**Q:** That's why they put you in to pinch run?

**A:** Oh yeah.

**Q:** Would they put you in on first base, or second base, or did it matter?

**A:** It didn't matter.

**Q:** Did you like pinch running?

**A:** Well, I watched pitchers a lot. I'd find out what their weaknesses were as far as people on base. You know, pitching is an art as far as pitching when people are on base. A lot of pitchers don't have that art. If you can pitch when there are men on base, you're a good pitcher. If you don't pitch well when men are on base, you're just an average pitcher.

**Q:** So, would they bother you much when they were out there?

**A:** They never bothered me.

**Q:** You were aware they were there?

**A:** I knew they were there, and I knew that if I kept them close to the base, that was my job.

**Q:** Did you have a good pick-off move toward first?

**A:** Not really. I had a better pick-off move to second base than I did to first. I'd just spin on my back foot and go.

**Q:** Did you ever hurt yourself sliding into second or third base?

**A:** No.

**Q:** When you slid, did you ever have to go in head first?

**A:** I went in head first sometimes.

**Q:** A lot?

**A:** Not all the time, no. It depended on how close the play was going to be. I could tell whenever the catcher was throwing the ball, or whether the pickoff play was coming, or what the situation was and how close the play was going to be. That determined how I was going into the bases—feet first or head first.

**Q:** And you never got hurt?

**A:** Not sliding. Not running into the catcher.

**Q:** Did you ever go in to home from third base and try to knock the catcher out?

**A:** Well, if he blocked the plate, and I was going in, and it was going to win the game, I'd run over him.

**Q:** Did you?

**A:** Yeah.

**Q:** Did you do it often?

**A:** As much as I could. I didn't want him to catch it more than I wanted him to pitch to.

**Q:** Well, you play the game to win.

**A:** That's right.

**Q:** Did you make any lasting friends on the team?

**A:** Oh yeah. I had one that, he and I were roommates for seven years, and we got along great together. I went to see him and he came to see me. It was Willard Nixon, down in Georgia (Red Sox pitcher, 1950-1958). He died from Alzheimer's. I hated that worse than anything.

**Q:** Did you like the fans? Did you like all that?

**A:** I never had them boo me, or say anything bad about me. I loved the fans. If you treat them like human beings, they'll treat you the same way.

**Q:** Did you enjoy the attention?

**A:** Yep.

**Q:** That leads me to the last question I'm going to ask you: Was it fun?

**A:** (Tom smiles broadly.) Yeah. I enjoyed the whole thing. Everything that I did I enjoyed.

**Q:** Good for you. You know, there's not many people in this lifetime who get to do what you did.

**A:** I know it. And I enjoyed it. There's not many people who had the privilege of playing like I did.

**Q:** Oh yeah. But you earned it.

**A:** Well, I felt like that if I could get up there and do my thing, I was going to do the best that I could to make friends, and to play the game like it ought to be played. And that's the way I played it.

**Q:** Let me turn this thing off. We're done.

**A:** (Tom laughing) Okay.

www.ingramcontent.com/pod-product-compliance
Lightning Source LLC
Chambersburg PA
CBHW021116020426
42331CB00004B/515